Bibliographic information published by the German National Library:

The German National Library lists this publication in the National Bibliography; detailed bibliographic data are available on the Internet at http://dnb.dnb.de .

Imprint:

Copyright © 2013 GRIN Verlag, Open Publishing GmbH
Print and binding: Books on Demand GmbH, Norderstedt Germany
ISBN: 978-3-668-07529-0

This book at GRIN:

http://www.grin.com/en/e-book/309177/exam-question-with-answer-expection-field-for-comperative-politics

Oliver Märtin

Exam Question with Answer. Expection Field for Comperative Politics

GRIN Publishing

GRIN - Your knowledge has value

Comparative Politics: Working Paper III.

Developing exam question out of the Curriculum of comparative politics

Conducted by Oliver Märtin

I. Imagine a non- faculty student asks you about the content of your student subject and wants further to know with which actors you are dealing in comparative politics resp. political science:

II. A) List at least five of them

B) Describe the working methods in the above mentioned respect

Answer Expectation Field

A)

➤ Government

➤ Lawmaker in a legislative body

➤ States

➤ Supranational organisations e.g. United Nations respectively multilateral Institutions e.g. OECD

➤ Private Sector

➤ Military

➤ Civil Society resp. civil movements

➤ Non-governmental organisations such as NGOs or grassroots campaign's

➤ Interest groups

➤ Policy makers

➤ Think Tanks

➤ Political Action committee's such as EMILY's List

➤ Political Super PAC's such as American Crossroad

➤ media

➤ Opposition ([within and outside of parliament]

➤ [Indirect actors] e.g. social media, trends in geopolitical tangential states or respectively cultural/ religious relative states.

B)

> Inductive approach

> Deductive Approach

> Case study:

> Descriptive theory.

> normative Theorie

> Comparative design: [most likely cases design and most different cases design]

III. A) Name the different kinds of democracies and the comparative electoral systems emerging from these different types. *Provide for every type at least one example:*

Answer Expectation Field

> **_Constitutional Democracies:_ First past the post** e.g. *United Kingdom or* **Proportional Representation** e.g. *Sweden, Netherlands, Denmark,* **Alternative vote respectively instant runoff voting** e.g. *Australia.*

> **_Direct:_** e.g. *free cities in ancient Greek and partially Switzerland complementarily to the government and parliament in Switzerland*

> **_Presidential:_ direct elections** e.g. *Argentina and with so most States in Latin America or* **electoral college** e.g. *United States]*

> **_Parliamentary_ First Past the Post** e.g. *India,* **_Proportional_ Representation** e.g. Germany, **Alternative Vote** e.g. Irland

> **_Mixed/ Semi Presidential:_ first part the post with a second ballot** France with a **simple first past the post system** Russian Federation during the era of Boris Jelzin [though in the post Jelzin era the Russian electoral system got reformed to a Parallel voting system and then finally to an entire Proportional Representation system], with a **parallel voting system** Ukraine and with **Proportional Representation** Germany during the Weimar Republic

B) Name the variety of democracies that may influence the outcomes in policy fields with strong land marking policy impacts in some systems and only minor outcomes in others. Underline every mentioned one with an example:

Answer Expectation Field

> Competitive, majoritarian "Westminster Type" [e.g. United Kingdom] vs Consensual negotiation type [e.g. Austria]

> Pluralism [Netherlands] vs neokorporatism [Russian Federation?]

> Centralism [e.g. France] vs Federalism [e.g. Federal Republic of Germany]

> Neoliberal [e.g. United States] vs Social Welfare States [e.g. Scandinavia]

IV. *Imagine you would work for an international think tank and writing an analyse on the new global super power China. From the communistic past [and presence] to the skyrocketing development of the Chinese economy – which struggles and challenges is facing China today, that could hinder their momentous rise on world stage?*

Answer Expectation Field

> *Multi – ethnicity*

> *Dangerous bulge of the male population as a result of the" one child policy"*

> Further population growth

> Income inequality

> Conflict between the fast developing urban areas and rural areas that are lacking troubling behind with respect to per capita income, opportunities and universal access to basic infrastructure provided by the very Chinese state

> Upcoming political protest

> A comprehensive dangerous level of pollutions with a deeply momentous concentrations on the Chinese metropolitan areas and their respective impact to health

> Resource depletion

> [rule of law and state monopoly of government] though nobody is serious contesting the authority and power of the Federal government within China [except from very small minorities and dissidents] the federal government cannot oversee totally the implementation of their adopted legislations e.g. the

environmental standards and protection got increased significantly, though implementation is lacking behind by the foreign and even more the original Chinese businesses' and industrial complex as well and insofar common law of the Chinese central federal government is often overturned by a "felt customary law" created by tradition in the Chinese periphery.

➤ Historic correlations that rising per capita income has led to more awareness and sensitive of the people on main street to values such as freedom, social policies, suffrage and participation regarding comprehensive public service policies and their consequences to the inner stability of the People's Republic of China.

➤ Brain drain of the young Chinese elites that are or were educated in the leading Universities of the west.

V.   Give at least three examples of social movements you know from history or presence and explain why they were or are important in order to understand country X

Answer Expectation Field

➤ *American's women suffrage movement*

➤ *Civil rights movement lead by Dr. Martin Luther King*

➤ *Conservative movements such as the tea party partriot*

➤ Starting with the last mentioned one: **The tea party patriots** together with **the tea party express** are fighting in their view to restore fiscal discipline and to react to "misguided stimulus spending" and to foster constitutionally limited government. Though they are official political independent – only republican lawmakers joined the tea party caucuses in the United States Congress. The tea party is fighting against the moderate- establishment wing of the Republican Party and is rejecting compromise aiming to adopt comprehensive legislation agreed on both sides of the aisles. They are fighting for less government, against the creation of quality affordable and accessible universal healthcare and especially the imperative mandate and are challenging with political amateurs the established republicans, who intend to run for higher public office. Often they could defeat their fellow republican friends in the GOP primaries and with so crusade e.g. sitting GOP senators in the land of the midnight sun, Lisa Murkowski in 2010 and former Delaware governor and Houseman Mike Castle got defeated in the GOP primary in the same year by tea party candidate Christine O'Donnell, whose campaign should later be covered in the history books "as one of the greatest possible disasters in the history of modern politics" and cost the GOP the House Seat plus a Senate Seat from the "Diamond state", that the RNC took for granted in order to take or respectively to hold on. Furthermore tea party candidates such Sharon Angle in Nevada [2010 Senate race], Ken Buck Colorado [2010 Senate race] and Richard Murdock Indiana [2012 Senate race] cost all together the GOP most likely the majority in the United States Senate. One of the biggest impacts out of the Tea Party movement is the Tea Party SOTU Response that is broadcasted complementarily by major American news cable to the official GOP response to the POTUS State of the Union address.

➢ **The suffrage movement** and the **civil rights movement** produced literally a sea-change within the history of the United States: The suffrage movement brought women the right to vote on a long march to share the same part of power like men. Hillary Rodham Clinton, whose mother Dorothy Rodham was born in a time that refused women's the right to vote, became the first serious female contender for the oval office [apart of Elizabeth Dole running in the GOP primary of 2000 against Bush 43] winning more votes in the 2008 democratic primary than any other contender for the highest office in the history of the United States and with so left 18. Million cracks in the remaining highest glass ceiling, which is hindering women to obtain the oval office and get equally empowered such as men.

➢ In a long run the suffrage movement also shifted ideas to the civil rights movement that apart from the fight for racial quality, also fought for women rights and once more it was Hillary Rodham Clinton, that stated at the ECOS summit, that founds it's footprint in history as the Beijing's UN declaration on women, her rejection of the back then UN principal to deal with the women issue separated from the human rights issue. HRC gave a historic speech with the worldwide most recognized line as it follows:" (...) If there is one message that

6

echoes forth from this conference, let it be that human rights are women rights and **women rights are human rights!"**

➢ The civil rights movement led to the abolishment of segregation and discrimination of African Americans in the American south, fostering the participation of Afro Americans in academia and the political process through affirmative action by e.g. creating congressional districts in the American south, where ethnic minorities are presenting the majority.

➢ Though until today the United States Senate remains a glass ceiling for Afro-American and women. Barack Obama was only the third **popular** elected Afro American to the United States Senate as he was sworn as Junior Senator from Illinois back then in January 2005.

➢ Before the year of 1992 [called the year of the women] there should never serve more than two female Senators in the same time in the upper chamber of congress. 1992 brought a game change to the so called most exclusive club in the world, when five female senators entered the upper chamber at the same time out off the1992 senatorial races and for the first time ever two female senators should serve as Co-Senator the constituency of their state – Diane Feinstein and Bambara Boxer – who served as chairs on the select committee of intelligence and the environmental senatorial committee until democrats lost the majority in the US Senate due to their midterm loss in 2013. The congressional delegation from the golden state also should later provide the first woman with the gavel of the speaker. And with so a dream for the post suffragette's movement should become literally true.

VI. What separates a potential fourth wave of democracy claimed in Huntington's scientific term from the previous waves?

Answer Expectation Field

➢ The digital revolution with respect to postmodern forms of communication and sharing of information within seconds from Buenos Aires to Quebec and from Wladiwosok to Lissabon and with so social networks such as Twitter or Facebook are creating a "post-modern -"domino movement," where the people from one country fighting the revolution are spreading the momentum to geopolitical, cultural and religious more or less close bordering nations.

VII. Essay question I: When will we see the first American President and the first female UN General Secretary shaking hands before an official joint press conference in the Rose garden:

Answer Expectation Field

Concept or resp. basic framework of the argument:

➢ Short history of the empowerment of women, dealing with the suffrage movement as mentioned above

➢ The first female lawmakers that have been married to their male husbands being lawmakers before

➢ Stereotypes that still hinder the women being put through the glass celling

➢ Cultural settings: Why are women more empowered in northern areas than southern areas e.g. almost factual gender equality in Scandinavia, German's first female governor – Heide Simonis – was sworn in the most northern region in Germany.

➢ Comparison to other states: Fernandez de Kirchner from Argentina and Dilma Vana Rousseff [Brasilia] being Commander in chief in Latin America

➢ Other global female very leaders such as Indira Gandhi and Sonia Gandhi in India and Julia Eileen Gillard [Australia] plus Ellen Johnson Sirleaf [Laureate of the Nobel Peace Prize]

➢ North America: Are Americans leading Women bicoastal? Why are the American states, that are sending two Madame Senators to the capitol largely bicoastal e.g. California, Washington state and New Hampshire plus Maine? Case study Olympia Snowe [being the first Woman elected to the state house plus state senate of Maine and then to the US House and Senate as well] and an additional case study about New Hampshire having an entire congressional delegation being female plus a female governor.

➢ When can we say: "Hello Madame President!"?

Most likely lawmakers being the first female President: Hillary Clinton, Elizabeth Warren, Kirsten Gillibrand, Key Alliote and Nikki Haley

> How long might it take till the community of nations will be lead and represented by the first female UN General secretary

VIII. *Essay question II: Imagine to be invited to speak as a European guest or exchange student before the UChicago Institute of Politics with its director David Axelrod and to prepare to hold a lecture there about "the European Union sui generis vs the American Exceptionalism:"*

Answer Expectation Field

> The EU is an incomplete political union being a case sui generis, while the US is a federal state lead by a federal government concentrating all competence in the field of foreign policy and national defence, while sharing the domestic competence with the 50 states And the territories such as e.g. Guam, Puerto Rico and American Samoa. For instance every American state has an own sales tax, while the federal government and the United States Congress have other rights in taxes e.g. extension of the Bush tax cuts. In contrast in the European Union, which is an incomplete federation of sovereign Member states, the EU don't can implement own taxes and has no competence on the tax issue outside of fostering a harmonization of standards with respect to tax rates such as the Sales tax or income tax.

> The exceptional historic path from the very founding fathers to the complete confederation of 50 states today lead to the establishment of one language and one culture [although there a big contrast on the heartland plus south and the West coast plus the historic liberal north east – while Europe is split into a huge ranch of individual languages and a different record of experience (both sides of the Iron Curtian, West Rome versus Byzantium eg. and different starting point [partial obliteration of society out of World war II]

> Similarities are as it follows: almost similar GDP, similar western culture (although oversea are different expectations about the role of the federal government, further similarity further similarity the paradox of rich vs poor voting patterns: in the European Union rich state with respect to per capita

9

income voting more left such as Scandinavia – while states with the poorest per capita income such as East Europe are predominantly lead by right parties, although with respect to the internal view of society in Europe – the economic poor Europe wide is endorsing left parties – while the economic advanced parts [except traditional postgraduates] are endorsing the center-right part of society. The same phenomena can be stated in the US: groups with less household incomes are voting for democrats, while very wealthy households often voting for republicans – but the richest states of the US [Except of Alaska because of special domestic energy income] such as the richest states Connecticut and Maryland [together with other East coast states and California] are deep blue, while in contrast very poor states in the American south such as Louisiana and Mississippi are predominantly republican [cause for this phenomenon the "cultural reproduction" of the economic elite in Europe like the US]

IX. Essay question III: Imagine writing a column for a political science paper such as the German "Politische Vierteljahresschrif" about, *what comparative Politics will be in the year 2050 all about:*

Answer Expectation Field

➢ How managed the BRICS States to become the leading power around the globe

➢ Demographic shift I in Germany: Turkish minorities path to political power – will there be a German head of State with Turkish roots?

➢ Will German or other leading states in the northern Hemisphere have the first open LGBT chancellor or Prime Minister

➢ Demographic shift in the United States, ethnic minorities [Latinos plus Afro Americans plus Asian Americans] will literally obliterate the white majority and dropt them from now 70% out of the population to the very minority. Case Study Texas becoming over time a purple and perhaps even a leaning blue state that will remind with respect to statewide voting pattern back on the time of the "Solid Democratic South" [although the increase will come entirely from the skyrocketing growing Hispanic Population in counties such as EL Paso and south Texas

➢ Transition of the European Union to the United States of Europe

➢ The study on the implementation of comprehensive reform on the UN security council

YOUR KNOWLEDGE HAS VALUE

- We will publish your bachelor's and
  master's thesis, essays and papers

- Your own eBook and book -
  sold worldwide in all relevant shops

- Earn money with each sale

Upload your text at www.GRIN.com
and publish for free